ACKNOWLEDG

I want to thank the Mighty God v
me to publish this book. God too.. ... through the
valleys and mountains of life to prepare me to
come up with the idea of putting my life
experiences and the power of God in a book.

I would like to thank all friends and family
members who read and edited the draft
manuscript. I value and appreciate their support,
willingness, and the time they took.

The Biblical texts used throughout come from the
New International Version (NIV)

May God bless you as you
read my experiences in this
devotional

Outalor

Table Of Contents

Introduction   3
God Has Plans   4
God Gives Rest   7
God Gives Power and Strength   10
God Supplies Our Needs   13
God Loves, and Nothing Separates Us from Him   17
God's Promises Never Fail   20
God Is with Us   23
God Is Faithful   26
God's Unfailing Love   27
God Gives Spirit of Power   29
God Our Strengthen and Helper   33
God Gives Wisdom   35
God Our Priority   37
God Honours Requests   40
God Fights the Battle   43
God Will Do It Again   47
No Shame   50
God Helps; No Need to Fear   53
God Guarantees Redemption   57
God Sends Angels   60
God's Unfailing Promises   63
God Renews Strength   66
God Gives Peace   68
God Delivers   71
God Gives Life in Full   73
God Is Present in Fire and Floods   76
God Gives More   79
God Will Wipe Away Tears   82

INTRODUCTION

This devotional is full of God's promises and my personal life experiences. God has done so much for me and what motivated me to write this devotional is how I have experienced God's power in my life. Although I have faced challenging circumstances, I have seen His power. In times of need, He provided; in times of storm, He stilled the storm and gave me peace; in the battles of life, he fought for me and won.

God has proved that He is real. He is not only the God of Abraham, Isaac, and all the other bible characters, but He is my God and yours. Therefore, God can do what He did in the time of Abraham and in the lives of all the men and women of faith who saw and experienced His power in the Bible.

Through my own experiences, this devotional aims to give someone hope in hopeless situations. I hope and pray that as you read this devotional, you will be encouraged to boldly claim God's promises and believe that He will fulfil these in your life. I encourage you to pray without ceasing. It may take time as God sees fit, but God is faithful.

DAY ONE
GOD HAS PLANS

SCRIPTURE: (Jeremiah 29:11)

For I know the plans I have for you, says the Lord, "They are plans for good and not for disaster, to give you a future and a hope."

DEEPER REFLECTION

I was born in Mberengwa, one of the districts in Zimbabwe. If the promise above had been told to my mother when I was born, she would not have believed it. I was born a sickly child. My mum said no one wanted to remain with me while she went to fetch water or do any other chores lest I die in their hands. As I grew up, I also realised how sick I was; I was always either at the local clinic or hospital. Due to my illness and the care nurses and doctors gave me, I decided to become a nurse to give back the care I had received. Unfortunately, my mother died when I was young and did not leave to see her daughter becoming a nurse in Zimbabwe and the UK.

My days in class were affected by the number of days I was sick, as I would miss a lot of classes. Despite missing classes, God gave me intelligence, which helped me perform very well. I passed my grade 7 exam with good grades. The expectations of my teachers and those of other pupils' were surpassed. My results got me a place for secondary education at an outstanding boarding school.

It was a Christian school, so it gave me a good foundation for my Christian life and the support I needed. From form 1 to form 4, I saw a significant improvement in my health. I believe God worked a miracle in my life due to the prayers offered for me by pastors and teachers.

God was faithful to His word. I passed my GCSE exam with good grades and got a place for nurse training. Having completed general nursing, I went on to do mental health and midwifery training. In all my training, I always got awards; for example, in General nursing, I got a shield for getting the highest marks in the final exam, and in mental health training, I got a medal for having the best research paper. I saw God's power in my life. Each time I made an achievement, my mind returned to my childhood experiences, which made me miss my mother very much.

I would have loved her to see the good plans God had honoured in my life. I can only imagine how proud she would have been of my achievements and the improvement in my general health and well-being. I am sure she would have told her testimony to many that God is above all kinds of illnesses. The community in which we lived thought that I was going to die in my early childhood life. As mentioned earlier, no one saw life in me but death; hence they did not want to partake in childcare when my mother was going to fetch water etc.

No matter what our situations may be like today, God has good plans for our tomorrow. Many people grew up healthy and did not achieve what I have achieved. I am a miracle, and no one in our family or community thought I could live up to 60 years. We serve an awesome God who can give life to lifeless situations.

I know God has good plans for me when it doesn't look like it, and He has good plans for you too. So keep trusting in Him. He is not a man that he can lie. (Numbers 23:19) God is not human, that he should lie, not a human being, that he should change his mind. Does he speak and then not act? Does he promise and not fulfil? I can testify that God is faithful and will accomplish what He has promised.

PRAYER

My prayer for you dear reader is that you will trust God with your future. He has it all planned for good. As you read and claim God's promises, He will honour as He promised

DAY TWO

GOD GIVES REST

SCRIPTURE: (Matthew 11:28-29)

Come to me, all you who are weary and burdened, and I will give you rest. Take my yoke upon you and learn from me, for I am gentle and humble in heart, and you will find rest for your souls.

DEEPER REFLECTION

This verse did not make sense when I read it before I had burdens. In 2006 my work permits expired, and I felt weary and burdened. In my mind, I could see myself going back to Zimbabwe. I left an NHS job to go to a private job because I believed I was facing discrimination. I had applied several times for courses that some of my colleagues were allowed to attend and had not been successful. I got frustrated and decided to make several applications. I got a job in a pharmaceutical company and found that the discrimination was much worse than I had experienced in the NHS. After three months, I decided to leave, which led to the termination of my work permit.

I needed a job as soon as possible to get a work permit. The NHS offered to take me back. However, I declined the offer because of pride and the thought of how I had been discriminated against in the past. I made several applications, and there were no job offers. My husband lost his job as he depended on my work permit. This was the beginning of problems as we had mortgages and bills to pay. I felt weary and heavy burdened, and all I could do was cry. Thank God for a prayerful friend who always encouraged and prayed for me. One morning I was reading a local paper when I saw an advert for a nurse at a nursing home, and I made a call. The employer called me for an interview which I passed, and I started work the following week.

I was excited but anxious as I had never worked in a nursing home. The owner of the nursing home was the manager. There was no flexibility with shifts. One had to work six half days and one-off, which meant that you were at work six days a week. I am a Seventh-day Adventist and was not allowed to be off on Saturday. Working on Saturdays was another heavy burden as I found it difficult not to attend church except on my leave days. Once again, I solicited prayers and made applications for a new job. Once more, God gave me rest from my weariness and burdens. I applied for work in NHS, was called for an interview, and got the job. This new job was a band six post, which was higher than band 5 when I left the NHS. What a mighty God we serve. God lifted my burdens and gave me a permanent job and a higher band.

Are you weary and heavy burdened? Whatever burden you have, God can give you rest. I pray that you will take all worries to God, who will honour His promise and provide you with rest. (1 Peter 5:7) Cast all your anxiety on him because he cares for you. It may take time as God sees fit but keep casting your cares upon Him, for He cares, and He will come through for you.

PRAYER

My prayer today is that you will take all your burdens to God and He will exchange with joy, peace and rest. May God give you rest. Things may be hard more than you can bear, feel or handle, do not be discouraged. God wants to give you the peace, joy and rest that you need. So lean on God and let God's peace flood into your heart. Remember God has not left you to face the problems alone. Life can be difficult but you are not alone.

DAY THREE

GOD GIVES POWER AND STRENGTH

SCRIPTURE: (Isaiah 40:29-31)

He gives power to the weak and strength to the powerless. Even youths will become weak and tired, and young men will fall into exhaustion. But those who trust in the Lord will find new strength. They will soar high on wings like eagles. They will run and not grow weary. They will walk and not faint.

DEEPER REFLECTION

In our lives today, we face stresses and strains due to economic difficulties, illness, relationship breakdown, and rebellious children.

With all this, we experience high levels of stress either from direct impact or due to the associated challenges in our work, personal life and family life. In times like this, we need God's strength, wisdom and resilience. And you must receive this from the Lord. Today we likely face more stressors and strains than usual as times in the world are brutal. Since we live in such challenging times with the economy, unemployment and the like, you are probably experiencing a high-stress level due to the associated challenges in your work, personal life and family life. During times like this, our level of strength, wisdom and resilience must be high.

And we must receive this from the Lord. In Mathew 7:7, God says to ask, and it shall be given to you; therefore, it is vital to ask God to provide us with power and strength in times of need.

One day we had to walk 5 miles with my sister to go and see my grandmother back in Zimbabwe in the rural area of Mberengwa. I was about six years of age. It was summer and very hot with temperatures of 40 degrees Celsius. I was tired and felt like I was going to faint. I also have been weak and tired even in my old age, so I understand what it means to be vulnerable and exhausted. Spiritually, I have had moments when I have been weary and tired of praying for a particular issue. I have felt like I have run out of strength. But, as the verse says, I have had new strength to keep trusting God through my prayers and intercessory prayers from friends and family. The only thing that keeps me strong is the prayers and God's power in my life. Amid storms, I have felt a peace that surpasses all understanding and have had strength restored. Reading God's word and promises have also given me the power to soar like an eagle.

PRAYER

I pray that today however weak you feel, you will trust that God can renew your strength and you will soar like an eagle. Keep praying, claim his promises and He will do that which he promised in

Jeremiah 33: 3 Call to me, and I will answer you, and show you great and mighty things, which you do not know.

DAY FOUR

GOD SUPPLIES OUR NEEDS

SCRIPTURE: (Philippians 4:19)

And this same God who takes care of me will supply all your needs from his glorious riches, which have been given to us in Christ Jesus.

DEEPER REFLECTION

In today's world, we are overwhelmed by sickness, negative news, violence and many other issues that make us anxious.

Anxiety can destroy our hope and faith in God. Sometimes we feel hopeless and feel like giving up on God when we do not have our needs supplied. There is no way you cannot be anxious about tomorrow when you lose a job, are diagnosed with cancer, marriage breaks down or goes through trying situations of need. The solution to all this is taking everything to God in prayer. As a nurse, I have nursed anxious patients who are nervous, restless, tense, tired and lost concentration. In times like these, one can quickly lose their faith and trust in God.

God promises us in (James 1:17) that every good and perfect gift comes from Him. What are the needs that cause you to be anxious today? Trust God, and He will supply them all. The key is to trust and believe that He will do so. If God can feed the birds that do not have fields, how can he fail to feed you or supply your needs today? The songwriter says, "All you may need he will provide; God will take care of you; Nothing you ask will be denied, God will take care of you. God will take care of you, through every day, o'er all the way; he will take care of you, God will take care of you." When hit by the storms of life, do not be anxious, but in everything, prayer and supplication with thanksgiving, let your requests be made known to God. (Philippians 4:7) says, "And the peace of God, which surpasses all understanding, will guard your heart and your minds in Christ Jesus."

I stand amazed at God's providence. He cares about even the trivial things we need today and the eternal blessings in heaven. In my time of need, I have seen God supplying all my physical and spiritual needs. In 2006 I lost my job, and my husband, who had a dependent visa, also lost his job. We had bills and mortgages to pay, and we were not sure how we would pay. However, God supplied miraculously. In our great need, our only hope was to trust in God and His word in providing for our needs. We remembered the verse in (Philippians 4:190) and claimed that God would supply all our needs. It was a difficult moment when we could not see a way out. All we could see was a house repossessed and us returning to Zimbabwe. The financial uncertainty meant we could not plan or do anything that needed money.

God provided a fantastic way. We used to pray for God to bless our groceries, and God answered as these lasted longer than expected. There was no month that we did not pay our mortgage, and there was no day that we had no food on our table. The savings we had, God blessed it and indeed provided all our needs. One day I saw a job advertised in the local paper, and I applied. I was called for an interview, got the job and was given a work permit. This meant that my husband, dependent on me, could also work. This journey taught us to trust God and His word.

PRAYER

I pray that you will trust God to supply your needs miraculously. You only need to trust God and call upon Him. In Philippians 4:6, Paul encourages us. "Do not be anxious about anything, but in every situation, by prayer and petition, with thanksgiving, present your requests to God". He also invites us in (1 Peter 5:7), "casting all your anxieties on him, because he cares for you" When we cast our anxieties in prayer, God reminds us that he is in control of every situation, and we will experience Peace in place of anxiety. There is no doubt that God knows and understands our situations and the debilitating effects of anxiety used as a weapon by evil when we cast our cares on God; our perspective changes from hopelessness to the possibilities God can do. Prayer calms our anxious thoughts and focuses our minds on a powerful

God and His precious promises.

Today take God at His word and take all your cares and anxieties to Him in faith. May God supply all your needs as He has promised in His word? He is not a man that He can lie. Trust Him and take all that burdens you to Him who can do beyond our expectations or imaginations.

DAY FIVE

GOD LOVES, AND NOTHING SEPARATES US FROM HIM

SCRIPTURE: (Romans 8:37-39)

"No, we are more than conquerors through him who loved us in all these things. For I am convinced that neither death nor life, neither angels nor demons, neither the present nor the future, nor any powers, neither height nor depth, nor anything else in all creation, will be able to separate us from the love of God that is in Christ Jesus our Lord".

DEEPER REFLECTION

This means that our fears for today, our worries about tomorrow, and that no power in the heaven above or on earth below can separate us from the love of God in Christ Jesus our Lord. What a powerful promise.

As I grew in my Christian journey, I realised that circumstances or situations could not separate me from God, my Father. There are times in my life that I have felt separated from God. Times when I fasted and prayed but received no answer. God seemed too far from me when I needed him to fight for me. Often, it is in these situations when I compare my life to my friends and family; it has mostly been material supplies. I never understood how God could be with me and not hear and supply my requests. Now I know that His love for me is eternal no matter where I am in life. Nothing will separate me from His Love. His love is deep. He sent His only son to come and die for me a painful death so that I can have eternal life (John3:16). There is no greater love than this.

Are there times of trials and temptations when you have questioned God's love for you? What are you going through today? Is it grief, job loss, divorce, or other trying situations? Take heart. God loves you and is the very present help. Look up to Him and not to your problem.

Count your blessings; name them one by one. Remember He sacrificed His son Jesus Christ to show His great Love to you and me.

God gives us another promise and assurance of His love for us in (Isaiah 54:10) "Though the mountains are shaken, and the hills are removed, yet my unfailing love for you will not be shaken, nor my covenant of peace be removed," says the Lord, who has compassion on you".

When I lost my mother and recently my sister, who was now like my mother, I felt separated from God. I could not understand how God could love me and allow my so-loved mother and sister to die so early in life. It is through prayer that I have understood these verses. It's incredible to know that NOTHING, even death, can separate us from the love of God. Reading His word and mostly my friends praying for me, I have grown to know God's, eternal love.

PRAYER

My prayer is that as you read this promise, it may be real in your life. May your trials and tribulations draw you closer to God? May nothing on earth and in heaven separate you from the love of God? All signs point to the soon coming of Jesus; therefore, hold on, my sister/brother. I pray that you may find the courage and the promise that Jesus gave us (John 14:1-2). "Do not let your hearts be troubled. You believe in God and also believe in me. My Father's house has many rooms; if that were not so, would I have told you that I am going there to prepare a place for you? Soon and very soon, we will see Him in the clouds coming to take us home where there is no more sorrow, and He will wipe away all tears.

DAY SIX

GOD'S PROMISES NEVER FAIL

SCRIPTURE: (Joshua 21:45)

"Not one of all the Lord's good promises to Israel failed; every one was fulfilled."

DEEPER REFLECTION

As the Israelites approached the Promised Land, Joshua reminded them of God's promise that He would bring them victory, help them defeat every enemy, and possess the land. But the closer they came to this land, the more they realised the size of the obstacles before them. They knew that victory would require many miracles. Some doubted that this was even possible. Yet, at the end of his life, Joshua reminded them that God had kept His promises. Humans may break promises for one reason, but God always keeps his promises. Marriage promises are some that have been broken. Broken promises have led to many heartaches, stress, and worst scenarios of marriage breakdown. One of the promises or wedding vows is "I…. take you …to be my husband or wife, to have and to hold from this day forward, for better or for worse, for richer, for poorer, in sickness and in health, to love and to cherish; until death do us part". Husbands or wives have broken this vow by having other relationships and failed to do as promised on the wedding day. This makes the other person feel betrayed. Many reasons lead to this, some of which may be as simple as lack of communication, commitment, culture, and religious beliefs.

Today we are like the Israelites who had journeyed 40 years in the wilderness and were approaching the Promised Land as we travel onto the Promised Land in heaven. God will keep His promises. Our idleness may be stress, weariness, tiredness, or sometimes bodily weariness, but too often, stress relationships, threats of things going wrong, overextending ourselves, commitments, lack of resources or any other. It does not matter where you are in your wilderness of life; God keeps His promises. So when we find ourselves low and discouraged and giving up on what God can do in these circumstances, this promise reminds us that God has a good plan, and His power never fails.

I have seen him keeping His promises in my life. He has provided, healed, sustained, given peace and hope, and delivered me from the devil's snares. When I look back over my life, I can see how God has kept promises in my life. This is why even when the devil throws stones at me; I will keep trusting God, the author and finisher of my life. I have learned it is His will for me when prayers have not been answered. God's promises are true for me, and you are today.

PRAYER

I pray that through the power of the Holy Spirit, God will open your eyes as He fulfils all His promises in your life. Doubt may keep you from experiencing God's blessings. Dear child of God, today, choose to move forward by faith, constantly trusting Him. Be faithful and obedient and see God keeping every promise.

DAY SEVEN

GOD IS WITH US

SCRIPTURE: (Joshua 1:9)

"This is my command-be strong and courageous! Do not be afraid or discouraged. For the Lord, your God is with you wherever you go."

DEEPER REFLECTION

These comforting words have applied to me and can be to everyone who seeks to live a good life and overcome our unique challenges. I have had moments of fear and discouragement in my life journey, and these words have comforted and strengthened me. At one time, I had an overwhelming job. Every morning I dreaded going to work to the point of being anxious and losing my confidence due to the work environment. In my leadership, I felt inadequate and overwhelmed by the behaviour and words of those I worked with. Was it not for prayers, encouragement from friends and God's word, such as this promise, I could have easily gone into depression?

God has been with me over the years and even today. When I am afraid and discouraged, God encourages me through His word and gives me peace that surpasses all understanding through the power of the Holy Spirit; the children of Israel had wandered in the wilderness for 40 years, and

Joshua had to lead them into the Promised Land. He was to claim the land from its current inhabitants, fight and lead battles and provide spiritual leadership for a large group of people. As he felt the task's overwhelming weight, the Lord offered these words of encouragement.

In my church leadership role, I have been discouraged and even given up some roles. I have also seen people refusing to take posts because of what they have witnessed or heard what others had gone through. Some have not taken leadership roles just because of fear of the unknown.

Joshua, having witnessed what Moses had gone through along the journey to Canaan, may have been discouraged from taking up the role of leading the children of Israel. The all-knowing God then came and gave him these encouraging words Are you overwhelmed by life circumstances, work pressures, church leadership pressures, maybe your children are giving you headaches, a husband who is into drugs and alcohol, a relationship strain with a sibling, a stressful job, financial challenges?

Whatever the cause of the weight that overwhelms you, God is saying this promise to you "This is my command-be strong and courageous! Do not be afraid or discouraged. For the Lord, your God is with you wherever you go." God is all-powerful and all-knowing. He has the answers and the strength we need to face any challenge before us. He was with Joshua and will be with me, and you are today. No situation, hurt, pain, disappointment, sickness, problem, condition, etc., is beyond God's reach. Trust Him today! Pray and keep believing as you boldly speak the word of God out of your mouth over whatever it is that you may be going through. If you have been discouraged, especially to take a role to work for God, please be encouraged that God will be with you as He was with Joshua.

PRAYER

I pray that you will not be afraid or discouraged but trust that God is with you through the valleys and mountains of life. May you feel the assurance that He is always with you.

DAY EIGHT

GOD IS FAITHFUL

SCRIPTURE: (Hebrews 10:23)

"Let us hold unswervingly to the hope we profess, for he who promised is faithful."

DEEPER REFLECTION

It is important to remember that God is faithful, not only sometimes when it's convenient, but He is always faithful. Sometimes we need to believe and trust that God can do small and big things in life.

In times of need, we need the assurance of this verse to remind us of an important truth. All we need to do is to hold onto God's promises and trust His faithfulness. When we do, we can move from constant doubt to uncompromising belief.

So the next time you begin to question or find yourself in a situation that seems impossible, know without a doubt that God is faithful. We can hold onto that promise today and every day.

PRAYER

I pray that the next time you begin to question or find yourself in a situation that seems impossible, know without a doubt that God is faithful. We can hold onto that promise today and every day.

DAY NINE

GOD'S UNFAILING LOVE

SCRIPTURE: (Isaiah 54:10)

"Though the mountains are shaken, and the hills are removed, yet my unfailing love for you will not be shaken, nor my covenant of peace be removed, says the Lord, who has compassion on you."

DEEPER REFLECTION

What a powerful promise to hold onto. Nothing changes the love of God.

This is awesome. Husband and wife exchange vows on their wedding day, and part of these is "till death do us part". This is how limited the love of a human being is. God's love goes beyond death. God loved us when he created us; He loves us today and for eternity. He has prepared mansions for us. In John 14:1-2, Jesus says, "Let not your heart be troubled; you believe in God, also believe in Me. 2 In My Father's house are many mansions; if it were not so, I would have told you I go to prepare a place for you."

God says through the mountains may be shaken, and hills are removed, His love will not be shaken. Can you imagine mountains being shaken? God keeps his promises; he is not a man that he may lie" God is not a man, that He should lie, nor a son of man, that He should repent. Has He said, and will He not do? Or has He spoken, and will He not make it good?" He promises to love you no matter what you go through. God's love is the one thing you can always count on. God's love will always be there regardless of the situation, no matter how you feel or what you have done. God's love never changes, never fails, and never ends.

God's love never changes. When our world is shaken, we can put our faith and trust in Him, knowing that His love will never change God's love is not based on your love for Him, your faith, your position, your sinfulness, your feelings, or any other condition you may think of God loves you because you are His child. He has engraved us in the palms of His hands. He says in Isaiah 49:15-16, "Can a mother forget the baby at her breast and have no compassion on the child she has borne? Though she may forget, I will not forget you! See, I have engraved you on the palms of my hands; your walls are ever before me."

PRAYER

My prayer today is that if you feel unloved by people of this world, you will call upon God, who can be trusted no matter what. You don't have to have any qualifications for his love. Remember His love for you never fails.

DAY TEN

GOD GIVES SPIRIT OF POWER

SCRIPTURE: (2 Timothy 1:7)

"For God did not give us a spirit of fear, but power, love and a sound mind."

DEEPER REFLECTION

What are you afraid of? Are you afraid of what the future holds? The prognosis of your illness is? The war in Ukraine and what it will result in? Or any other causes of concern? I understand that we live in a hostile world filled with pain, discrimination, unfairness, hate and death.

According to the Oxford dictionary, fear is ". The emotion of pain or uneasiness caused by the sense of impending danger, or by the prospect of some possible evil. "I am sure each one of us has gone through this type of emotion. Each time a certain occurrence comes, it causes fear within me; for example, when Covid 19 came and was causing death to so many people. My fear was I was going to survive. I lost close friends and family members during the pandemic, and it stirred fear within me. I feared I could not meet my family in Africa again when locked down. It seemed as if there was no hope for this pandemic to end. When the pandemic God better, the war in Ukraine erupted.

During the pandemic, people lost jobs, fearing the future, with some taking their lives as if they had no hope. Marriages and relationships were broken, abuse increased in the homes, mental health illness increased, and drug and alcohol misuse increased. Most of these issues may have been caused by the thought of a bleak future and, for example, would take alcohol and drugs to cheer themselves. Recently war broke out in Ukraine, and many of us are afraid of what this war will result in. I have heard some say that it's likely to be a world war 3.

When you watch the news and see the destruction and killings, it's hard not to be afraid, especially if you are in Ukraine or have family there. The desperation and crisis are unbearable and make it difficult for a human being not to be afraid. How can you not be afraid when you hear bombs or guns in your neighbourhood? Humanly it's difficult, but with God, it's possible not to be afraid but to trust God. The fear of someone with a relationship with God differs from that of someone who doesn't know God. When you have a relationship with God, you rest in His promises and the knowledge that even if I die, there is an eternity in heaven. You face death with the hope of a future, unlike someone who does not know God, who believes death is the end.

God, in His wisdom, knew that in this world, His people would be afraid at one time or another.

This is why He gave us the Spirit spirit of power and a sound mind so that we can stand firm and fearless in these bad times. God has given us the Holy Spirit, who makes us fearless in troubled times, works His power in our weakness, and fills us with courage, hope, strength and a sound mind in harsh circumstances.

In my fearful times, I thank God for knowing Him and for having a prayerful group of friends and family. We pray and encourage each other in the word of God. I also individually pray on my own and tell God my fears. I do not know your fears today, but I can assure you that if you take them to God, He will give you the spirit of power, love and a sound mind. He will give you peace in a troubled situation. He will give you courage and the strength to face the circumstance. The devil will tell you there is no hope in trusting God, the all-knowing and powerful. He has given me peace and power to overcome fearful times, and He can do it for you. Be encouraged by His promise in Joshua 1:9 "Have I not commanded you? Be strong and courageous. Do not be afraid; do not; Be discouraged, for the Lord your God will be with you wherever you go." You may be asking, where is God in all this? The answer is He is with you as He has promised in Joshua 1:9

PRAYER

I pray that God will give you the spirit of power, love, and a sound mind. May He give you the peace that surpasses all understanding that no man can give in Jesus' name.

DAY ELEVEN

GOD OUR STRENGTHEN AND HELPER

SCRIPTURE: (Isaiah 41:10)

"So do not fear, for I am with you; do not be dismayed, for I am your God. I will strengthen and help you and uphold you with my righteous right hand." In this world, there are so many things that may cause us to feel afraid and weak. Jesus in John 16:33, "I have told you these things, so that in me you may have peace. In this world, you will have trouble. But take heart! I have overcome the world."

DEEPER REFLECTION

When the Covid 19 pandemic hit the world, many of us were afraid and are still afraid as we saw so many people dying, including our close relatives. The doctors we looked up to were helpless seeing so many people die under their care. No one could help us or strengthen us.

Money could not help as Covid 19 virus killed the poor and the rich. It is in this crisis that many of us would have loved to hear these words. In our fear of death, to hear God say do not be afraid. I remember when I had a major operation here in the UK, and the only close person I had was my husband. It was scary and frightening thinking of the unknown. We had just migrated to this country and had no friends except work colleagues. I was so afraid that if anything happened to me, how would my husband cope? With the pain I experienced, I was losing hope. I was so weak that I could not walk or able to do activities of daily living on my own. I had to depend upon nurses. My hope was in God, and this verse gave me hope and strength for the future. The verse brought comfort, peace and assurance, knowing that God has told me not to be afraid and promised to strengthen me in my time of need. God's presence in my life was the greatest thing that drove the fear away from me during my distress. When times are tough, God will give you the strength to make you stronger and fearless in Him.

PRAYER

Dear reader I pray that today you will not be afraid or dismayed, as God is by your side and has promised to uphold you with His righteous right hand. He is a very present help for you today, right now.

DAY TWELVE

GOD GIVES WISDOM

SCRIPTURE: (James 1:5)

"If any of you lacks wisdom, you should ask God, who gives generously to all without finding fault, and it will be given to you".

DEEPER REFLECTION

Wisdom is essential in life. I have made many unwise decisions and choices in my life journey. I didn't make the decisions and choices to God but in my wisdom. The results have been disastrous and, in some cases, suffered the consequences. One of the unwise decisions I made was trying to do business in Zimbabwe while in the UK. Money was spent, but nothing materialised. The reason that led me to the loss and non-progress of the business is that I did not depended on God's wisdom. I had relied on what I saw other people do and what others said regarding business at the time. The unwise decision was that I had the opposite result of what I had hoped for. In my mind and plan, I thought that if I had business in Zimbabwe, I would not need to make money when I went home. Instead, I thought I would use money from the business and take care of the family in the same business. The truth is that I did not get even a penny out of this. Had I taken this to God in prayer, He would have stopped me from going ahead, and I would have saved money and my heart from the pain of loss.

Have you ever made unwise decisions? Today the promise is that if we ask for wisdom from God, He will give us generously.

PRAYER

As you make decisions, I pray you will involve God, who gives wisdom and direction. God knows what is best, the beginning and the end are in His hands, so you can trust His wisdom.

DAY THIRTEEN

GOD OUR PRIORITY

SCRIPTURE: (Mathew 6: 33)

"But seek His kingdom and righteousness first, and all these things will be added to you."

DEEPER REFLECTION

In my prayers, I used to ask the opposite of what Jesus said in this verse. I remember telling God to bless me with money, material things such as houses and luxurious things. God, in His wisdom, taught me the correct way of requesting by not honouring my selfish requests. This was a very difficult lesson as I had served God for the wrong reasons. I thank God that He took me through the wilderness of life for me to learn that what matters in life is not material things but the kingdom of God.

While I sought to be rich and acquire material things, God took the money away from me and left me a place of need for Him than material things. I got poorer in my quest to get rich as I lost money in the adventures. I tried running remotely a transport business that took a lot of money and brought nothing in return. I tried several other businesses that failed; I believe because God wanted me to come to a place where I could seek His kingdom first.

God was second to what I searched for in this journey of seeking material things. Anxiety and fear of the future ruled my life. In all I was doing, I was preparing for my retirement. In my heart, I would have acquired enough wealth in retirement to live comfortably. God, in His grace, woke me up from my dream of searching for earthly riches to the reality of seeking His kingdom first. I realised that it makes sense for me to seek God first and trust Him with my present and future because He is the one who created me, knows my needs, and supplies them.

The promise of supply is on the condition that we seek His kingdom first. When we seek God's kingdom first, we trust that God will care for our needs no matter how things look. Seeking God's kingdom first means we believe that God is the creator and sustainer of life. We often lose sleep seeking earthly materials, yet God has all planned for us. In the early church, the believers did not worry about earthly materials after the outpouring of the Holy Spirit. They brought the materials for use for the advancement of the kingdom of God. This is what seeking the kingdom of God is about, when our concern is not about getting rich as I did but seeking to advance God's kingdom. God then supplies our needs. Money and earthly treasures and prosperity do not need to be our priority but God's kingdom and righteousness.

It's easy to let anxiety rule in our hearts and get all

twisted up with many concerns about how our needs will be met. Jesus tells us not to worry, and for a good reason. The Father knows our needs and has promised to take care of us. Our job is to lay all our anxiety, worry, and fear at the Father's feet and seek His kingdom, trusting that He will take care of us just like He promised.

"But seek His kingdom and righteousness first, and all these things will be added to you. This promise means that when you put your trust in God's and His way of doing things first, all the other concerns of life will fall into place. You can experience the peace of knowing that God will supply all your needs. God takes care of all your life's concerns when you put His concerns first.

PRAYER

My prayer today is that you will choose to seek the kingdom of God and His righteousness first. It may take some time before all your needs things in life are supplied by God but know that in time He will make sure that all the things you are concerned about are taken care of.

DAY FOURTEEN

GOD HONOURS REQUESTS

SCRIPTURE: (Mathew 7:7, 8)

"Ask, and it will be given to you; seek, and you will find; knock, and it will be opened to you."

"For everyone who asks receives, and he who seeks finds, and to him who knocks, it will be opened."

DEEPER REFLECTION

I remember in my childhood asking my parents to buy me a pair of shoes and a dress for Christmas. The answer to my request was that they did not have money. I was very disappointed as I was looking forward to putting on the dress and shoes and going to church. I did not know that my parents had already bought me a dress and a pair of shoes but would give them to me on Christmas day. I spent the time before Christmas angry and disappointed, but this changed on Christmas day when I realised that they had bought a more beautiful dress and pair of shoes than I had requested. This is the same with God. He knows what is best, and when we ask, He may not give us, but as He promised at the right time, He will give us what is best.

For many years I have asked, sought, and knocked on heaven's door. My mistake has been that I did not do this according to God's will. I have asked, sought, and knocked on the door for selfish reasons. The Bible says in 1 John -21 22, "Dear friends, if our hearts do not condemn us, we have confidence before God and receive from him anything we ask; because we keep his commands and do what pleases him." If we keep His commandment, we will ask, and God will give us, and James 4:3 says when you ask, you do not receive, because you ask with wrong motives, that you may spend what you get on your pleasures". This verse opened my eyes, realising I had been selfishly asking God for my pleasures.

I have learnt to trust God when I ask. I now can have peace within my heart even when I do not get the answer knowing that God is my Father, and He knows what is best for me. I am His daughter, and He knows when to answer me and how to answer. God want us to seek Him and His righteousness first. In Amos 5 vs 4, the Lord says to Israel: "Seek me and live. Not seeking earthly treasures but seek God who will supply these when you knock on heaven's door; God will open for you through Jesus. John 14: 6 Jesus answered, "I am the way and the truth and the life. No one comes to the Father except through me. This means having a relationship with Jesus Christ, who is the way or door to the Father.

PRAYER

My prayer today is that as you ask, seek, and

knock, you will do so for the glory of God through Jesus Christ. Keep asking, seeking and knocking without ceasing and in due season, he will answer, you will find, and the door will be opened for you.

DAY FIFTEEN

GOD FIGHTS THE BATTLE

SCRIPTURE: (Exodus 14: 13-14)

Moses answered the people, "Do not be afraid. Stand firm, and you will see the deliverance the Lord will bring you today. The Egyptians you see today you will never see again."

"The Lord will fight for you; you need only to be still."

DEEPER REFLECTION

After the children of Israel had been delivered and were on their way to Canaan, the army of Pharaoh followed then. They were surrounded by mountains, and before they were the Red Sea. In human terms, this was a difficult situation, and as the army of Pharaoh drew closer and closer, their fear increased. They started accusing Moses of taking them out of Egypt to die. They forgot how God rescued them from slavery and brought them out with wealth. They also forgot the miracles that happened before their deliverance. The children of Israel's faith in God, who had promised to take them to the Promised Land, disappeared and fear and despair took over.

The above passage of Exodus 14: 13-14 is a response of Moses to the fearful Israelites who could not see any way out of their situation. They could not turn back as the army was pursuing them or forward as they could drown in the Red sea. All they could see was their death. With the threatening waves of the Red Sea ahead, mountains around them and the chariots of Pharaoh's army drawing closer and closer, fear and doubt wiped their confidence in God's promise of His presence and protection in the cloud by day and a pillar of fire by night. Moses then came with the reassurance, "Do not be afraid. Stand firm and see the deliverance the Lord will bring you today. The Egyptians you see today you will never see again. The Lord will fight for you; you need only to be still."

Have you ever been in such a situation? I have been in several situations that challenged my faith in God when I took my eyes off Him and focused more on the problem. Like the children of Israel, I saw the enemy pursuing and the Red sea before me. Thank God for my friends like Moses, who directed me to a God who is mightier than my enemies and reminded me of His promises. Exodus 14: 13-14 were some of the verses they quoted for me, uplifting me and redirecting my mind to the mighty God.

My immigration status changed in 2006, and I faced deportation back to Zimbabwe, where I needed to go back and apply for a work permit. In Zimbabwe, I faced the possibility of my permit not being renewed and facing economic challenges. Days drew closer and closer when I was required to either get a work permit or return to Zimbabwe. I had made several applications, all of which were declined. I continued to pray and asked my prayer partners to pray for me. They all encouraged me to believe in God and His promises. One day I phoned after coming across an advert for nurses to whom I applied, and God came through for me and won the battle.

Crossing the Red sea showed me that God has higher ways of delivering his people. Who would have thought that water could have thought that the sea could be divided into two walls and people walk on dry land?

Are you in a place where you cannot see your way out? God has many ways of fighting our battles. Ways that we may not know until He does it.

Read the Bible to get encouragement from such stories of the Red Sea crossing and pray and believe that he will fight to victory no matter how difficult our fable minds may tell us.

PRAYER

In your battle, I pray to focus on God and His promises. All His Promises, He will honour, so today, claim His promises upon your life. Remember, He is God who does not change. Just as He rolled the waters of the Red Sea and made way for the Israelites but had their enemies drown, He will do it for you and me in our battles. In Deuteronomy 1:30 (NIV), God has a promise: "The Lord your God, who is going before you, will fight for you, as he did for you in Egypt, before your very eyes."

DAY SIXTEEN

GOD WILL DO IT AGAIN

SCRIPTURE: (Deuteronomy 1: 30-31)

"The Lord your God, who is going before you, will fight for you, as he did in Egypt, before your very eyes, and in the desert. There you saw how the Lord your God carried you, as a father carries his son, all the way you went until you reached this place."

DEEPER REFLECTION

This promise is repeated along the way. In Deuteronomy 3:22, Moses reassures Joshua as he is about to take over the leadership "Do not be afraid of them; the Lord your God himself will fight for you. "Moses again is reminding the children of Israel of how God again would fight for them." In Deuteronomy 20:4, the children are encouraged that in war, God was going to fight "The Lord your God is the one who goes with you to fight for you against your enemies to give you victory."

This was a promise to the children of Israel as they journeyed from Egypt to Canaan. They were to look back and see what God did in Egypt, and this was to encourage their faith in God, who did wonders in Egypt for them and had the power to do the same. The promise was that the God, who went before them in a pillar of cloud by day and a pillar of fire by night, would fight for them. Although their enemies were greater and taller, God was higher and stronger than the enemies.

These promises are relevant to us today; I have witnessed the wonders of God fighting for me in my own life. I have had enemies fighting with me and have seen God fighting for me. In 2007 I had a car accident, which was not my fault but the other driver's fault. He was driving a posh Mercedes Benz, and I was driving a Peugeot 323. At a roundabout, he came and hit me on the side. He was supposed to give way but was speeding, so I think I could not apply the brakes in time. We stopped, and he started accusing me. He did not listen to me. He did not want to exchange details. As we were arguing, the highway police patrol arrived and asked us to get out of the roundabout, which we did. I took his registration number and a photo of the damage he had caused. I informed my insurance of what had happened when contacted; he denied that it was him who was in the wrong, and the case went on for some time. The solicitor took the case to court in Essex, where the accident happened, and I lived in Surrey. There was so much for 2 miles on the day that it took more than an hour.

The M25 was very busy, and we drove less than 40 miles per hour. I arrived at the court 2 hours later. When I reported, I was told that the gentleman did not turn up for court, so the case was judged in my favour.

What a mighty God we serve. I did not have to attend the court, but God attended on my behalf. Although I arrived late, God judged in my favour.

The gentlemen who appeared to be a good person or rather was against compared to me was fought and defeated by my God. This reminded me of the battle between Goliath and David. Goliath thought he was to crush him because he was a giant and David was a small, inexperienced boy. He did not know that David had a greater man who fought for him. Mathew Henry, in his commentary, says, "Our plans seldom avail to good purpose; while courage in the exercise of faith, and the path of duty, enables the believer to follow the Lord fully, to disregard all that opposes, to triumph over all opposition, and to take firm hold upon the promised blessings".

What battle are you fighting today? The God who has been leading you until today will fight for you.

PRAYER

My prayer is that God will remind you of what he has done for you in the past and give you the confidence that He will fight and win this battle. Your strong and giant enemies are no match for our God. Take everything to God in prayer, and you will be surprised what He can do.

DAY SEVENTEEN

NO SHAME

SCRIPTURE: (Psalms 34: 5)

"Those who look to him are radiant; their faces are never covered with shame".

DEEPER REFLECTION

David is confident that the Lord protects and delivers all who fear Him and will not be ashamed. Radiance is great happiness which shows in someone's face and makes them look very attractive. Some of the synonyms are happiness, delight, pleasure, and joy.

I must confess that I have found it difficult to be radiant when faced with trials, needs, concerns and tribulations. However, I have remained focused and trusted in God, believing that the season will come to pass. Indeed by His grace and power, I have come through the other side with radiance on my face.

Through my journey, I have learnt that looking up and trusting in God makes one experience peace and joy instead of despair and hopelessness. When one focuses on circumstances, they appear big and overwhelming but looking to Him in every situation brings peace, and when people look at you, all they see is radiance. If we look to God, our burdens are removed from our hearts, and our faces become radiant with hope, peace, happiness and joy.

In my life, I have had people asking me if I ever get stressed sometimes at a point when I am burdened and overwhelmed by problems. I am sure there is something they saw in my face. Maybe a happy or radiant face, although I would not be feeling so.

There is a difference between a person trusting in God and the one who does not trust in God, although they may be facing exactly similar situations. As the verse said, the one who trusts God their appearance is not appeared gloomy or covered in shame and dejection but instead is radiant. While one without God will complain and blame their situations on other people etc., the one who trusts in God will praise Him in prayer and songs. They experience peace, joy and happiness instead of despair and hopelessness. This is because the one who trusts in God does not look at their circumstance but at God, who changes situations. On the other hand, the one who does not trust in God looks and dwells on the problem and ends up being overwhelmed to a point in some cases of being suicidal or even committing suicide.

PRAYER

My payer is that you will have the confidence in God that no matter what challenges may come your way, He will not let you be put to shame. He is loving, all powerful and there is nothing too hard for Him to do. All you need today is to surrender and trust and He will transform your situation and give you a radiant face. God's promises are true. Present your case to God and claim His promises today. Today may you lift up your eyes, above your circumstances and challenges you are facing and look up to God? He is your hope and salvation who can solve your problems.

DAY EIGHTEEN

GOD HELPS; NO NEED TO FEAR

SCRIPTURE: (2 Chronicles 32:7-8)

"Be strong and courageous, be not afraid nor dismayed for the king of Assyria, nor for all the multitude that is with him: for there be more with us than with him."

"With him is an arm of flesh, but with us is the Lord our God to help us and to fight our battles. And the people rested themselves upon the words of Hezekiah king of Judah."

DEEPER REFLECTION

Sennacherib, in 2nd Chronicles 32:15, says, "Now, therefore, do not let Hezekiah deceive you or mislead you like this, and do not believe him, for no god of any nation or kingdom was able to deliver his people from my hand or the hand of my fathers. How much less will your God deliver you from my hand?" This promise came to Hezekiah and Judah's children, whom Sennacherib threatened.

It may not be a physical war but an emotional, spiritual, or psychological one. There are Sennacheribs today who are threatening us today. The Sennacheribs are work, illness, unemployment, marriage, disharmony, or any other circumstances threatening the children of God. You may feel threatened by the situation you are in today, but there is a God who sends angels to fight for us victoriously, In 2 Kings 6:17 (NIV), when the Syrian army surrounded the city, Elisha's servant was frightened, and we read in verse 17 "And Elisha prayed, Open his eyes, Lord, so that he may see. "Then the Lord opened the servant's eyes, and he looked and saw the hills full of horses and chariots of fire all around Elisha".

I remember when the devil threatened me with losing my work registration. If I had been found guilty, it would have meant that I would be struck off the register, and I would not be able to work as a registered professional.

The story is that on a particular day, I was at work when I gave a strong injection for pain. I gave the injection in the presence of my colleague, as is required by the policy. In a hurry to go and give the patient the pain killer as he was groaning with pain, I forgot to lock up the cupboard where the injections are kept. As I returned to the room where we keep the injections, I found one of my colleagues there, and she told me that I had left the cupboard unlocked. She explained how serious the case was. I tried to explain that the patient I had gone to give the injection was groaning in pain, so I genuinely forgot to lock up and that I had come back straight after giving the injection, so I was going to lock up anywhere.

When I saw that she was serious, I reported this as an incident according to the policy. I also phoned the duty manager and explained the incident. The manager asked if I had written an incident, to which I answered yes. She did not comment anything, so I thought the case was finished but little did I know that my colleague had communicated with the manager and told her that I had left the cupboard open, and I only got to realise when she told me. The manager phoned me and said that she had been informed that I had not realised I had left the cupboard open. I explained the side of my story, but a conclusion had been made, and both the manager and my colleague wrote to my professional body for me to be investigated for incompetency. I only got to know it when I received a letter from my professional body two weeks after the incident.

I told my friends and family to pray as I responded to the letter. Like Sennacherib, the person had threatened my livelihood, but I trusted in God as Hezekiah, and God fought for me. After investigations, it was found that I had made an error and was honest and managed the issue according to the organisation's protocols. I was therefore acquitted. God fought the battle for me. While they wrote against me, I had many who were invisible on my side. God sent angels who wrote positive reports and fought the battle for me, and the battle was won as He promised in Chronicles 32:7-8. After the investigation, it was found that I had no case to answer. What a mighty God we serve.

When you rely on God and trust Him to fight for you, you will have peace in the battle and grow closer to God in the process. You may not face a literal army, as Hezekiah did, but may face battles at work, home, or school. Hold fast to your faith and pray to God; who will you fight and win the battle for you?

PRAYER

My prayer today is that you will be strong, courageous and not afraid of armies of disappointments, challenges at home and work, marital problems, illness, death for there are more on your side than on the enemy's side. March with a song of praise trusting that God who never fails will transform your situation today.

DAY NINETEEN

GOD GUARANTEES REDEMPTION

SCRIPTURE: (Isaiah 44:22)

"I have swept away your offences like a cloud, your sins like the morning mist. Return to me, for I have redeemed you."

DEEPER REFLECTION

As the clouds are of different shapes and colours, so are our sins. They separate us from God. Isaiah 59: 2 "But your iniquities have separated you from your God, your sins have hidden his face from you". While our sins may be different, they all separate us from God. The murderer, thief or just a negative thought about someone are all sins that separate us from God. No sin is greater than the other. However, the good news is that the moment we place our faith in the Lord God and give Him our lives and confess our sins, we receive complete forgiveness for all that would have separated us from having a good relationship with our heavenly Father. We are guaranteed of our sins being blotted as promised in Isaiah 44:22. In life, we may at the past struggle along the course of our lives, but the good news is that God's mercy never fails; his compassions never run out. Lamentations 3: 22 "Because of the LORD's great love we are not consumed, for his compassions never fail. They are new every morning, great is your faithfulness."

Robert Robinson is a man who composed an SDA hymn number 334.

In his 4th stanza, he wrote:

> *O to grace how great a debtor,*
>
> *Daily I'm constrained to be!*
>
> *Let Thy goodness, like a fetter,*
>
> *Bind my wandering heart to Thee.*
>
> *Prone to wander, Lord; I feel it,*
>
> *Prone to leave the God I love,*
>
> *Here's my heart, O take and seal it,*
>
> *Seal it for Thy courts above."*

This should be our daily prayer and song. We are prone to wander from the close relationship with our God in our daily life journey.

Whether you have wandered a few steps from God or miles away from Him who redeemed you, be assured that He is ready to receive you back in His arms when you turn to Him with a surrendered heart. On Calvary's cross, the sin of all our sins are forever blotted away; Ellen G White, in her book Steps to Christ (SC 52.3), writes, "None are so sinful that they cannot find strength, purity, and righteousness in Jesus, who died for them. He is waiting to strip them of their garments stained and polluted with sin and to put the white robes of righteousness; He bids them live and not die."

This is the great hope we have. In my life journey, I have sinned and wandered away from God. I have been encouraged by this verse, and I pray every day as I wander and ask for forgiveness; he never fails me. He gives me peace that surpasses all understanding. I used to condemn myself and think that God would not forgive me for what I termed big sins.

PRAYER

My prayer today is that no matter how far you may feel you have wandered from God, come, and he will take you in His loving arms. The devil will condemn you, but God calls you to abundance, love and life eternity. Your sins are not greater than His love, in fact it's the opposite.

DAY TWENTY

GOD SENDS ANGELS

SCRIPTURE: (Psalms 34:7)

"The angel of the Lord encamps around those who fear him, and he delivers them."

DEEPER REFLECTION

The above verse reassures those who fear the Lord of an Angel in those camps around them and even delivers them from any harm and danger. In today's world, so much can harm or endangers us. Gun crime is increasing globally, and every day we hear of innocent people being killed, the latest being school children in America. There is war in most parts of the world which is killing innocent people, and recently we are witnessing the war in Ukraine, where many have been killed, injured, displaced, and families separated. There is an increase of different illnesses that have killed and are killing many people, for example, Cancer, Covid 19 and all others. In such a world, those who fear the Lord will find comfort knowing God dispatches an angel to encamp and deliver them. All these issues may threaten us with mortality and disability and rob us of safety, peace, joy and socialisation. No one wants to live in such environments where there is no hope for tomorrow, and people live in constant fear.

During the first wave of the Covid 19 pandemic, some people in high-risk areas left their jobs, and families protected themselves by exercising enhanced personal protective measures.

The impact of war and illnesses leads to Post Traumatic Stress Disorder and many other psychological symptoms such as depression, anxiety, loneliness etc. During the Covid 19 pandemic, there was a rise in mental health disorders, drug and alcohol use, divorce, and domestic violence.

This is when one needs the assurance of an angel encamping and delivering them from the trouble.

On numerous occasions, I have been delivered from a situation in miraculous ways. This has made me believe more and more that a band of angels always watch over us and is around us to help when we are in need. One day after I bought my new car, I was unaware of how it worked. I managed to drive off the driveway to go to work. However, when I got to a place where I needed to reverse, I did not know what to do. There were cars behind me, and I was becoming nervous and anxious. At that time, I did not think to pray as my mind was now worried about the people behind me.

As I was still trying to figure out, God sent an angel as a human being who was kind to help me. The lady in question was also not very knowledgeable, but she remembered that her husband's car was like mine and suggested what I could do. I did it, and indeed it worked. While some may have been angry at me for blocking the way or delaying them, God sent someone to deliver me from the situation that could have easily deteriorated into insults.

God has angels waiting to assist and deliver His children. It is amazing how God loves and cares for us. In her book My Life Today, Ellen G White, p304, writes, "Angels come to our world. Nor are they always invisible. They sometimes veil their angel appearance; as men, they converse with and enlighten human beings."

Prayer

My prayer is that when faced with a challenging situation, you will call upon God, who is ready to dispatch angles to help you. Psalm 34:7 says, "The angel of the Lord encamps around those who fear him, and he delivers them." I pray that you will feel safe knowing that God cares for you and is ready to support you.

DAY TWENTY ONE

GOD'S UNFAILING PROMISES

SCRIPTURE: (Joshua 23:14)

"Now I am about to go the way of all the earth. You know with all your heart and soul that none of the good promises the Lord your God gave you has failed."

DEEPER REFLECTION

Joshua took over leadership from Moses and, just before his death, delivered his last address to the people. He was among the people who witnessed miracles God performed during the plagues, deliverance from the Egyptians, the crossing of the Red Sea, manna in the wilderness, and defeat of the Amalekites, while Moses interceded for their victory.

Joshua remembered the covenant that the Lord made with the children of Israel. At the point where he felt he was going to die, Joshua wanted to stress God's goodness, faithfulness, and long-suffering.

He wanted them to look back and see how God had fulfilled His promises from deliverance in Egypt to the Promised Land. I have often been tempted to focus on the negative things that have happened to me in life. I have found it easier to remember the storms of life than the blessings, and I am sure many of us have found it easier to remember more the negatives than the positives, and yet if I were to count one by one, the positives would be way much more than the negatives. The negatives have often been due to my wrong decisions and not involving God in the plans or decisions. Just like the children of Israel, the enemy sometimes defeated them because they had not listened to God.

Joshua, at this time of the end of his life, did not highlight the problems that they had had along the way from Egypt to Canaan but God's faithfulness that he wanted them to remember, "not one thing has failed of all the good things which the LORD your God spoke." Not one word of God's promises of blessings on our lives has failed. In Deuteronomy 31: 6, God has promised never to leave or forsake us.

Due to the business of life, sometimes we do not pause to count our blessings and name them one by one or to pause and consider how God came through for us in our lives, the protection from wars, pandemics, accidents, and so many other things that could have occurred us.

God is the same yesterday, today, and forever. We serve a faithful God who keeps all His promises. The same words said to the children of Israel are relevant for us today, and we can trust Him to keep all the promises he has made.2 Corinthians 1: 20 says, "For no matter how many promises God has made, they are "Yes" in Christ. And so, through him, the "Amen" is spoken by us to the glory of God". God never changes in this world which is ever-changing. He is not changed by our unfaithfulness, failures, or circumstances.

PRAYER

My prayer today is that you will focus on God and not a circumstance that clouds the goodness of God and the wonderful things he has done for you. He has given your life in a world where so many are passing on, protection from the arrows of the devil, family, job, and so many other blessings I have not included. May God, through the power of the Holy Spirit, always reveals His love and faithfulness. The most important thing is that the same promise to the children of Israel can be personalized to you and me today. You know with all your heart and soul that not one of all the good promises the Lord your God gave you has failed". Numbers23:19 says, "God is not human, that he should lie, not a human being, that he should change his mind. Does he speak and then not act? Does he promise and not fulfil? When you remember this, I pray that you will start to praise God in joy, sickness, trials, and tribulations, knowing that God never fails."

DAY TWENTY-TWO

GOD RENEWS STRENGTH

SCRIPTURE: (Isaiah 40:31)

"But those who hope in the Lord will renew their strength. They will soar on wings like eagles; they will run and not grow weary; they will walk and not be faint."

DEEPER REFLECTION

I have had difficulties that have devastated me with fears for my life and the future. I must admit that there are times when my heart has grown faint and weary. Times when I have stumbled and fallen because I relied on my strength, wisdom and resources that have proved insufficient to give me strength in the storms of life. I have learned that only the power from God is sufficient to sustain me and keep me running without getting weary and faint. When I have turned to God in times of need, He has given me the strength to keep focusing and trusting in His strength and power. During the pandemic, I lost many friends and relatives, but the worst was when I lost my sister, who was like my mother and her son-in-law followed in less than a year. I had no strength and was weary, filled with hopelessness and anger towards God. My sister was a prayerful woman who trusted in God. On the day of her death, we had sung in the morning and prayed. She then had a prayer and praise with her children from around 10 to about 1400 hours, when she asked her daughters to let her lie down and rest. At about 5min, my sister quietly and peacefully rested in the Lord. She had been unwell for some time, but this did not take away her faith in God, who was faithful and gave her strength to run in the race of illness without getting weary. She ran the race of life without getting weary of trusting in God in her pain.

As we run our races in this world, what we need to soar with wings as eagles are faith in God and trusting that God will bring to pass the promise that He will give the strength. His grace is sufficient for us, no matter how weary we may be, for His power is perfected in our weakness. Our God is faithful and true to His Word and satisfies our lives so that our youth is renewed like an eagle. He is going to those who wait for Him and seek Him - trust Him and love Him. God will lift us on eagles' wings and carry us through life's stresses and strains in the power of His Holy Spirit. The Holy Spirit enables us to run the race and win in His strength, win the prize in heaven.

PRAYER

My prayer is that today you will hope in the renewal of your strength and that you will not be tired but soar like an eagle no matter how much the devil attacks you.

DAY TWENTY-THREE

GOD GIVES PEACE

SCRIPTURE: (John 16:33)

"I have told you these things so that you may have peace in me. In this world, you will have trouble. But take heart! I have overcome the world."

DEEPER REFLECTION

Can one find peace in this world filled with sorrows, illnesses, wars, trials, and tribulations? Jesus, when He was about to die, He reassured His disciples that even if this world is full of trouble, He gives peace, not as the world gives. The world gives temporary peace, but He gives everlasting peace. God's peace means even in troubled times, one has inner peace. The world's peace is brought by the absence of, for example, wars, illnesses, etc. This is why people do not find peace in the world.

In my country, there was once a war, and everyone was praying that the war would end. In1980, my country gained independence, which was the war's end. However, this has not given the people peace as so many other things bring troubled hearts, such as unemployment, illness, and homelessness, to mention a few. While people expected independence to give them peace, this has not proved so.

Money is one of the things that people think if only

they can get, they will have peace. I came to this country in search of monetary peace, but today 20 years later, I have not found peace. Yes, I have had a better salary than in my home country, but this has not brought me peace; if anything, the reverse is true. Covid 19 brought global chaos of illness and death in the last two years. Covid 19 did not discriminate between rich countries from developing countries, the rich and the poor, the educated and uneducated, everyone was affected, and people lost close friends and family members. I also lost friends and family members, and work colleagues. I know families that lost five family members one after the other, both parents dying, leaving young orphans.

Peace is one of the fruits of the Spirit spirit. In this world, nothing gives internal peace as cost-of-living rises; unemployment is rising, marriages are breaking down, conflicts between individuals, families and nations, disasters, and diseases. The solution to having peace during the above is having a relationship with Jesus, who will give you peace, not as the world gives but the peace that surpasses all understanding. The Peace that Jesus gives is the peace that will keep you calm and focused when everyone around is perplexed and overwhelmed by the events of the world. Many have developed mental health illnesses, such as I am reminded of a story recorded in Mathew 8:23-27 and Mark 4:35-40. When Jesus was asleep, a great storm arose, and the disciples were afraid. Even though they had seen Jesus perform miracles, they panicked as they thought they would die. Jesus rebuked the storm and said peace be still, and it was so. Jesus can say peace be still in the storms of our lives, and we will experience the peace that surpasses all understanding.

PRAYER

My prayer for you today is that you will only look up for peace that is from God as He will give you true peace not as the world gives.

DAY TWENTY-FOUR

GOD DELIVERS

SCRIPTURE: (Psalm 50:15)

"And call on me in the day of trouble, I will deliver you, and you will honour me."

DEEPER REFLECTION

In my life, I have trusted my late sister to tell her all that troubled me. When my mother died, she took over the responsibilities of a mother. I could call her any time of the day, and she would respond. Sometimes she would have a solution to my problem, but most times, we would just pray. After migrating to this country, her help and support were limited to calls and advice. The truth is after her death, I could not call unto her\and that meant that I had no one to help.

In Psalms 50:15, the omnipresent God invites us to call on Him when in trouble. Unlike my sister, who was limited in the help she could give, God will deliver us whenever we call him. God wants us to bring our troubles to him when we need help. He will give us victory, deliverance, and peace during our trials. In this promise, we need to do something for God to respond. God calls us to call Him when in trouble. Not that we should only pray when in trouble, but when in trouble, just like a child to a dad, we need to call Him. We do not need to find our solutions as we are limited, but God knows the best solution for us. God promises that when we have called, He will deliver us. Oh, what a promise. We are not called to do extraordinary this but to call Him and tell him of our troubles, and He will deliver us. We are assured of deliverance from our troubles with no condition. This is a promise, and God is not a man that He may lie. When God has delivered us, we will honour him. In the Bible, we are reminded to do all things for God's glory. 1 Corinthians 10:31 "So, whether you eat or drink or whatever you do, do it all for the glory of God".

Today reflect on how many times you were in trouble and did not call on God but on someone else. Days of troubling me in different ways; it may be marriage breakdown, cancer, Covid19, death of a loved one or loss of a job. The list is endless, but whatever it may be, calls on God who will deliver you, and you will honour Him. This is a missed opportunity to honour God because when problems are solved, we focus on the person God has used instead of honouring him.

PRAYER

I pray that you will call upon God in your small and big problems, who promises to deliver you from them all. Before calling upon the pastor, friend or relative, your first port of call should be God.

DAY TWENTY-FIVE

GOD GIVES LIFE IN FULL

SCRIPTURE: (John 10:10-11)

"The thief comes only to steal and kill and destroy; I have come that they may have life and have it to the full.

"I am the good Shepherd. The good Shepherd lays down his life for the sheep."

DEEPER REFLECTION

I have had stories and experiences of people who come to steal and kill.

In today's world, robbers use guns and will come and take your hard-earned money or property at gunpoint. Either they kill you, or you let them take what they want. If you want to defend yourself, they may kill you and take all they want. I have read stories of families who were visited by robbers who tied all the family members and threatened them with death if they resisted. Thieves or the devil do not care about human life. The devil has come to kill and destroy. Every day we see and read how people are shot and killed in their homes, schools, shops etc. There is war everywhere, and nobody seems to care about death which is everywhere.

The good news is that we have a good Shepherd,

Jesus Christ, who looks after us. He has come to give us life in abundance and not to kill us. As a good shepherd, He laid His life for us. Every day He watches over us, protects, provides and is always waiting for us to run to Him for all our needs when the devil pursues us. Jesus came from heaven to die for us. Today He is interceding on our behalf in heaven. Jesus suffered from our behaviour. He was beaten, spat, mocked, and nailed to the cross. The good news is that after three days, He arose, and He lives today to defend us in our helpless situations. He calls us to go to Him so He can shepherd us as the devil will offer us nothing except to kill and destroy us. The devil will use wars, diseases, drugs, and alcohol to kill and destroy us. Jesus, on the other hand, gives us His tender love and compassion. When we are lost, He is willing to go after us until we come back to the fold. His love is everlasting.

PRAYER

My prayer for you, dear reader, is that you may give your life to Jesus, who fully gives life. The one who is the good Shepherd, as David said in Psalm 23. You will not want any as he will provide all your needs. He will guard over your life and protect you from harm and danger. It is reassuring to know that God your Shepherd will provide for you, and you don't need to worry about anything. He provides all your needs, such as rest, food, guidance, friendship, comfort, joy, peace, goodness, mercy, and many other needs of this world.

DAY TWENTY-SIX

TITLE: GOD IS PRESENT IN FIRE AND FLOODS

SCRIPTURE: (Isaiah 43: 2)

"When going through trials and tribulations of life, one may feel like you are on fire or drowning in deep waters. God promises that when the fire threatens to burn us and the waters threaten to drown us, He will be there to ensure they don't. Our God is a great God who always has a way out and ready to save your life."

DEEPER REFLECTION

In Exodus 14, the Israelites had an experience of what God can do when faced with a crisis. They were faced with the Red sea ahead and the enemy perusing them. Who would have thought that the sea cans part\and waters dividing into pillars on either side, allowing the Israelites to pass on dry land as if there was never a sea before? Can you imagine the fear and hopelessness that could have gripped their hearts on being faced with the sea before them and the enemy behind them, and the mountains around them? It must have been a terrifying moment; hence they started to complain and wished to be in the land of slavery than die in the desert. In Exodus 14:13-14, Moses answered the people, "Do not be afraid. Stand firm, and you will see the deliverance the LORD will bring you today. The Egyptians you see today you will never see again. The LORD will fight for you; you need only to be still." God made a way by having the angel, in a pillar of cloud, stand between the Israelites and the army of Pharaoh, protecting God's people.

Moses stretched his hand out over the sea, and God caused a strong wind to blow, parting the waters and changing the God-made sea floor into dry land. God made a way where there was no way, and the Israelites crossed the Red sea while the enemy drowned. Similarly, in Daniel 3, Shadrach, Meshach, and Abednego experienced God's power in protecting them from the fire. In the hour of their trial, when they were thrown into a pit of fire, they remembered and trusted God's promise in Isaiah 43:2 "When you pass through the waters, I will be with you; and when you pass through the rivers, they will not sweep over you. You will not be burned when you walk through the fire; the flames will not set you ablaze". God, in His faithfulness, honoured His promise, and the three were not burnt despite being in a pit of fiery furnace that had been heated seven times hotter.

The Lord, who made way for Israelites in the sea and a path through the mighty waters, and protected the three Hebrew boys from burning, is the same God who today can see us through our fires and Red seas. He can perform the same miracles he did at the Red sea and in the fiery furnace. All we need is to look up to Him and trust Him. When faced with challenges, we often become fearful, but God in this passage tells us not to be afraid as He will always be with us.

The sadness and pain in today's life call for a faith that will not waver but ad the people of old call up to God, who hears and answers. We need to show the world around us that He is the only God we worship.

Like in the days of Shadrach, Meshach, and Abednego, today, at the end of earth's history, the Lord will come through for His children who do His will. He who walked with the Hebrew boys in the fiery furnace will also be seen in our crucibles. His love and abiding presence will comfort and sustain us in our difficulties. In our fiery furnaces, as we look up to God, trust Him, and stand firm in our faith, we will not be moved to the right or the left. The Angels that excel in strength will protect us, and God will reveal Himself as God above all gods, able to save and deliver those who trust Him.

PRAYER

My prayer today is that no matter the depth of your water or the extent of the fire you are in, you will not be moved but trust in His word. Our God, I can strengthen and help you in every situation. In Matthew 19:26 (NIV), Jesus said, "With man this is impossible, but with God all things are possible". Nothing is impossible with him.

DAY TWENTY-SEVEN
GOD GIVES MORE

SCRIPTURE: (Malachi 3:10)

"Bring the whole tithe into the storehouse, that there\may be food in my house. Test me in this," *says the Lord Almighty, "and see if I will not throw open the floodgates of heaven and pour out so much blessing that there will not be room enough to store it."*

DEEPER REFLECTION

God is the giver of everything, including life, health, a sound mind, family, jobs, and many other blessings. He is the creator of all things, including us. God is very generous with all the blessings; hence, we take life and all the resources He gives us for granted. When God created Adam and Eve, He entrusted us with all things. He created the earth and everything in it and entrusted us to care. After creating Adam and Eve, He put them in the Garden of Eden. Genesis 2:15 says He "took the man and put him in the Garden of Eden to work it and take care of it."

In Leviticus 27:30, God says, "A tithe of everything from the land, whether grain from the soil or fruit from the trees, belongs to the Lord; it is holy to the Lord." Proverbs 3:9 says, "Honour the Lord with your wealth, with the first fruits of all your crops.

This means that for everything God blesses us with, we should give a tenth to God. God requires this for the advancement of His mission. By returning tithes faithfully, we obey God and acknowledge that all comes from and belongs to God. He challenges us to give and see if He will not open the the\windows of heaven and pour out blessings so that there will not be enough room to store them. This calls for a step of faith, to believe and trust that no matter our financial situation, if we give a tenth to God, He will open heavens flood gates of blessings.

I got to understand tithe after I was married and went to my husband's church, where I worship up to now. Initially, I did not believe that when I paid tithe, God could open the gates of heaven. After studying the Bible on this topic and discussing it with the pastor and other members, I realised that it's not only money that God will bless us with but many other blessings. I decided to give my tithe and made a covenant with God that I would be faithful to pay tithe every month. The truth is it's easy to do so when one is in financial health. I came to a time when I was not getting enough money and decided not to pay tithe and bills. This made life very difficult for me as money was insufficient during the months, and I did not pay my tithes. When I paid my tithes, I realised I received many blessings; for example, friends and family would bring food or money. I also realised that just a small amount of food would take much longer than expected. Since my lesson during my time of need, I have not stopped paying my tithes. I have experienced God opening the flood gates of heaven and blessing me above imagination.

PRAYER

Dear reader my prayer today is that you will be encouraged to take God at His word you to try our faithful God with tithes and see how He will bless you. He has promised and will do it because He is not a man who will lie. Number 23:19 says, "God is not human, that he should lie, not a human being, that he should change his mind. Does He speak and then not act? Does he promise and not fulfil? What He has spoken, He will fulfil. He is not a man that He can lie.

DAY TWENTY-EIGHT

GOD WILL WIPE AWAY TEARS

SCRIPTURE: (Revelation 21:4)

"He will wipe every tear from their eyes. There will be no more death, mourning, crying, or pain, for the old order of things has passed away."

DEEPER REFLECTION

I find it difficult to imagine a world where there will be no suffering, no crying, no pain, and no death. To imagine that I will live in a world filled with joy, peace, happiness, and all the good God has prepared for us makes me long more and more for that land. Because the word of God says so, I believe so.

In this world, I have been pained, cried and death robbed me of my loved ones. If tears could dry, mine would have dried. I lost my mother many years ago when I needed her most. She was suddenly taken from us. The grieving and pain took many years, and even today, there are times when I miss her very much and cry a lot. My mother and aunt died a few days between and were buried one after the other. It was a dark moment, and no one could tell me that there was a world where there would be no death or pain. I was filled with sorrow and loss and disappointment and blamed God for allowing my mother and aunt to die so young and leave us behind.

Over the years, I have lost close relatives, friends, and colleagues. On 28th August 2020, I lost my eldest sister, who had assumed my mother's role from the time my mother died until her death. I was heartbroken and was taken back to when my mother died. My sister was a woman of great faith, and in the life, we lived together, she mentored me and taught me what it means to be a Christian. In her challenges, she always prayed and believed in God's will to be done. She was unwell for some time, and in her pain, she had faith in God and was ready for whatever His will for her life was. She asked for me the night before her death, and her daughter called me. We spoke, sang her favourite hymns, prayed, and said good night. I phoned her the following morning, and we sang and prayed once again. I was so happy as my sister sounded much better. In the afternoon, as I talked to a friend explaining how happy I was as my sister was much better, I received a call from her daughter to say she had passed. I cannot explain the pain that gripped me. I cried inconsolably, but nothing changed. When I read

Revelation 21: 4 I wished the world could end and we go to the wonderful place where God would wipe away our tears, and there will be no more death to rob us of our loved ones.

I am encouraged by the promise in Isaiah 43:18-19 18 "Forget the former things do not dwell on the past. 19 See, I am doing a new thing! Now it springs up; do you not perceive it? I am making a way in the wilderness and streams in the wasteland". God spoke to Isaiah so that the children of Israel would not focus on their past failure, sin and discouragement and look forward to God's new plan for them.

This promise speaks to us today in our wilderness of life. He is making away and streams along our way. Thank God for the new thing that God is making in our lives. I can't wait to witness the new Heaven and Earth with former things that have passed away. The new place with no sorrow but a time to rejoice and celebrate with our loved ones.

This will be our destination. No more night, no more pain, no more death, no more separation or anything that pains the heart. Imagines ting in the mansions that our Lord Jesus Christ promised. Nothing will separate us again, not even death. Death will lose its power. Our Lord

Jesus Christ came and died for us so that we may finally be with Him, Father God, Holy Spirit and the host of angels and enjoy the life God intended for us from the beginning.

PRAYER

I pray that you look forward to a new Heaven and

Earth where God Himself will wipe away our tears. Dear reader, trust God in your time of pain and sorrow that He will make a new thing in your life.

May you find comfort in knowing that one day this world of sorrow will be no more? Today you may not see any hope because of the pain you are in and the state of the world, but take heart that a day of rejoicing is coming. The wars and senseless killings will be over, Covid 19, Cancer and all the bad things happening around will be over. We will see our God face to face and be able to share our stories and forget our painful past. In the new heavenly home, there will be joy, peace, and happiness forever and ever.

Printed in Great Britain
by Amazon